COMPUTERS

Library of Congress Number: 84-9792

4 5 6 7 8 9 10   98 97 96 95 94 93 92 91 90 89 88

Library of Congress Cataloging in Publication Data

Zomberg, Paul G.
   A look inside computers.

   Includes index.
   Summary: Explains how computers, especially micro-
computers, work, traces their history, and discusses programming.
   I. Bond, Bruce, ill.   II. Title.
QA76.23.Z66   1984   001.64   84-9792
ISBN 0-8172-1409-7

COMPUTERS

By Paul G. Zomberg

CONTENTS

RAINTREE PUBLISHERS
Milwaukee

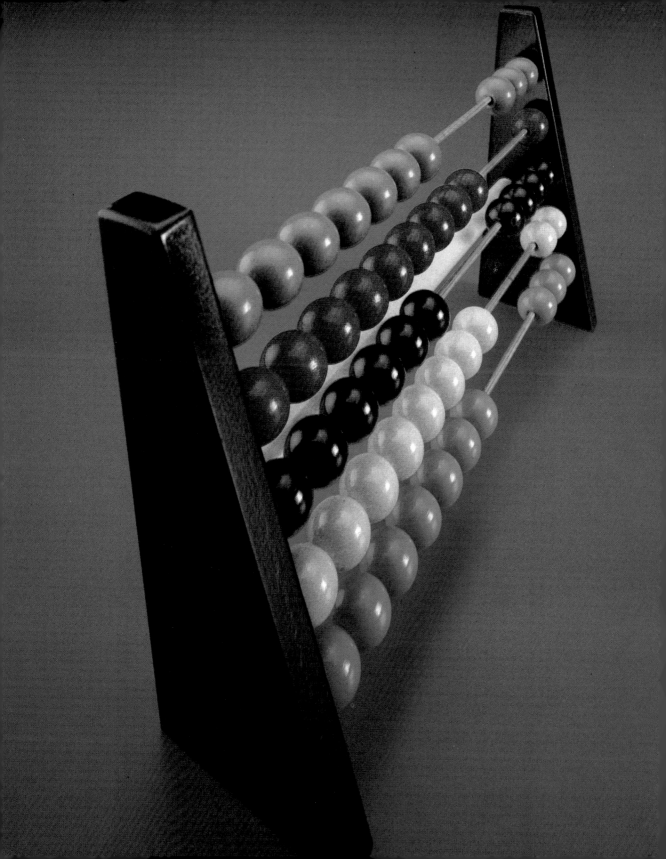

COMPUTERS

Computers can be found just about anywhere. They're in homes, offices, and schools. They can be seen in people's laps as they ride in trains, buses, planes, and cars.

People of all ages use computers. Some use them to solve very complex mathematical and engineering problems. Others use computers to write newspaper articles, ads, magazine stories, and even books like the one that you're reading. Computers also keep track of things for people—money, parts, other people . . . just about anything that can be counted.

And, of course, people use computers to play all kinds of different games—from chess and logic games to shooting down imaginary alien vehicles from space.

Computers that people use today do the same things that other machines and people have always done. They store information; they retreive information; and they process information. When a computer

An abacus is an example of an ancient computer. From the earliest of times, people have used machines to help them to do mathematical calculations.

5

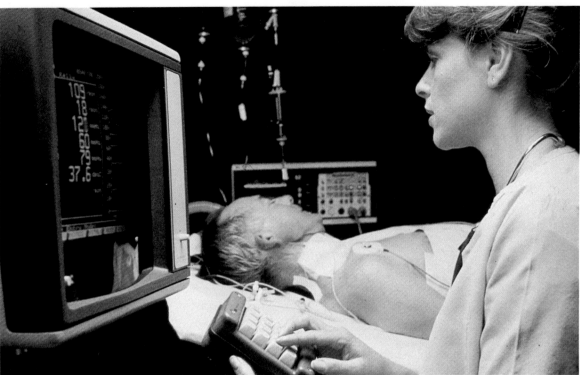

Patients in hospitals can be watched closely with the help of computers. When the patient's condition is critical, computers alert the staff when immediate care is needed.

stores information, it keeps the information so that it can be used later. No matter what kind of computer it may be, it can hold information.

And then you can find the information again—retrieve it. So, in a way, a piggy bank is like a computer—you save pennies in it, and then can get them out when you need them. You can store and retrieve pennies.

But a piggy bank cannot process pennies; it cannot solve problems with them. Computers can solve problems. They might be simple math problems like:

$$12 + 39.06 + 16.59 - 6.32 =$$
$$12,356 \times .14 =$$
$$15.6 \times (126 \div .10) =$$

More than likely, however, the problems are quite complicated. And they're not always math problems. Computers can be used to find houses, prescribe medicine for sick people, and deliver news, weather, and sports information.

Computers are valuable for keeping track of parts in a warehouse. A computer can tell its operator the location of thousands of parts and where they are going.

THE HISTORY OF COMPUTERS

The history of the computer begins with people searching for ways to perform complicated calculations with numbers. The abacus is an example of a machine that was invented to do just that. An abacus can calculate arithmetic problems. Abaci have been used in many parts of the world since ancient times.

Very early mechanical computers consisted of numerous gears and cams. Mechanical clocks, which date back as far as the 9th or 10th century, are examples of computers designed to measure and count units of time.

In 1834, a British mathematician named Charles Babbage designed a mechanical calculator. It was capable of doing math problems accurate to twenty decimal places. Babbage's machine was a *digital computer* called the Analytical Engine. The Engine was designed to receive information in the form of punched cards. However, construction of it was never completed.

In 1834, Charles Babbage designed a mechanical calculator that was called the Analytical Engine. It was a digital computer.

In 1855, a Swedish manufacturer used Babbage's design as the basis for a mechanical calculator. During the next one hundred years, mechanical calculators came into common use as adding machines, cash registers, and billing machines.

The next major step in the development of the computer was to use electricity to power the machines. Electromagnetic relays and vacuum tubes were used to do the work instead of gears, cams and levers.

In 1939, John V. Atanasoff and Clifford Berry designed a digital computer that used vacuum tubes and capacitors. They built it so that it could solve equations used in the science of physics. The computer is called the Atanasoff-Berry Computer (or ABC).

The ABC computer was the inspiration for a much larger one. It was constructed in the early 1940s. It was called Electronic Numerical Integrator and Computer—or ENIAC, for short.

John Mauchly built ENIAC in Philadelphia for the U.S. Army. The ENIAC consisted of hundreds of large metal cabinets, most of them filled with electronic relays and vacuum tubes. It consumed a large amount of electricity, gave off a great amount of heat, and filled several rooms at the University of Pennsylvania's Moore School of Electrical Engineering. Some people thought that six ENIACs would be as many computers as the world would need.

The Sperry-Rand corporation acquired rights to build other ENIACs, calling them UNIVACs. A new kind of expert, called a computer scientist, came into existence.

Computer scientists were a small, select few at first. They were the ones who gave us such words as *byte* and *input* and *software*. They gave us other words as well. When a moth got caught in a mechanical relay of an ENIAC one day, the computer would not operate. Eventually, the moth was found and removed, and the computer worked fine

Early computer hardware was more difficult to handle than today's hardware.

again. Before long, any fault in a computer or a program was being called a "bug," and correcting the problem was called "debugging."

In 1948, the transistor was invented. A transistor could do the same thing that a vacuum tube could do, but it needed very little electricity, was far smaller, lasted longer, and gave off hardly any heat. A digital switch on a computer now took up one-tenth of the space required of the relays that had been used before. Computers, radios, and many other electronic instruments became smaller in size, thanks to transistors. It soon became possible to reduce the size of a computer to the point of taking up about as much room as two office desks. A computer of such a

size is often called a "mainframe."

During the 1950s data-processing equipment used eighty-column punched cards. International Business Machines (IBM) made people familiar with the cards. The machines used to process the cards were very large, and each machine could do only one task at a time: punch the cards, sort the cards, or print the information on the cards. Some of the machines could be "programmed" by circuit boards, which were wired by hand.

The punched cards were a convenient way to record and store information. But the process of handling the cards and getting information from them was quite slow. Electronic computers changed everything.

An electronic computer could record and store large amounts of information and quickly make it available. And a computer program could do the same thing as the hand-wired circuit boards.

The size of computers continued to shrink during the 1960s. At the same time, their

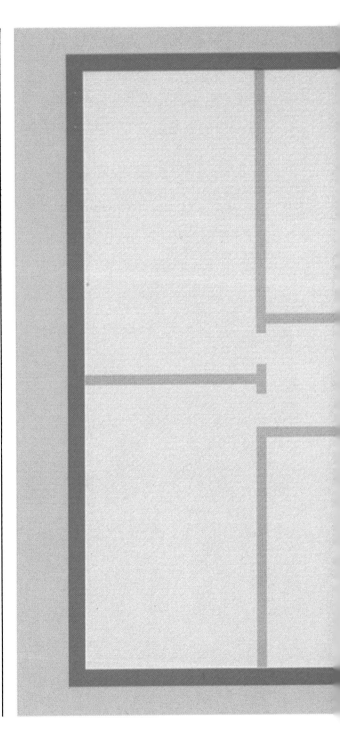

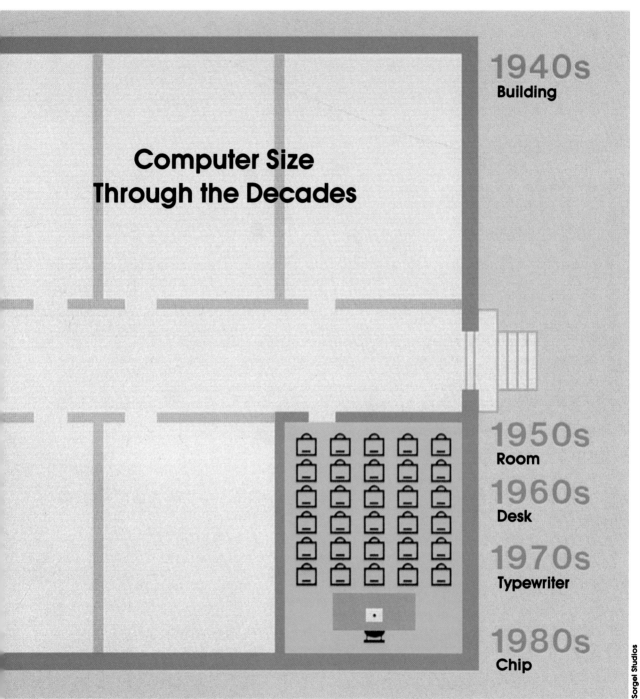

Computer Size
Through the Decades

1940s
Building

1950s
Room

1960s
Desk

1970s
Typewriter

1980s
Chip

13

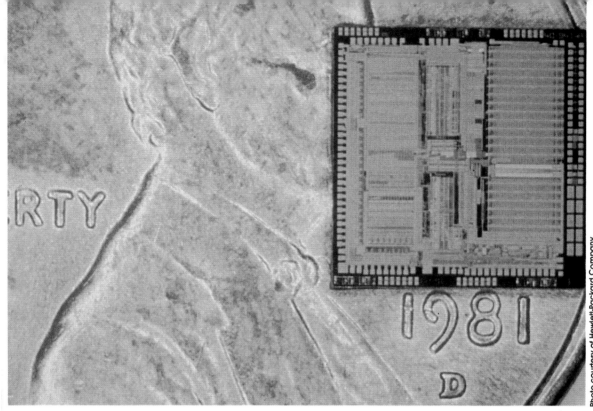

Photo courtesy of Hewlett-Packard Company

A new computer chip with 450,000 transistors is as powerful as the room-sized computers of the past.

capabilities continued to increase, thanks to the development of *integrated circuits* (ICs). Like the transistor, an IC is a semiconductor. That is, it can switch from being a conductor of electricity to being a nonconductor and back again. An IC switch was one-tenth the size of a transistor switch. The smaller, file-cabinet-size computers that used ICs were called *mini*computers.

The trend toward smaller computers continued during the 1970s. The invention of the silicon *chip*—a miniature electronic circuit containing the equivalent of thousands of ICs in about one square inch—meant that the central part of a computer could be even smaller. The entire *central processing unit* (CPU) could be "engraved" on one chip. The *micro*computer (also called a personal computer, or desktop computer) was born when the CPU and memory circuits of the

Computers are used to show models of machines, like NASA's space shuttle.

minicomputer could be put on a single six-by-ten-inch circuit board.

The first commercial microcomputers were available in the mid-1970s. By the mid-1980s, the microcomputer's potential for uses in business, education, science, manufacturing, and entertainment had become very evident. The cost of a microcomputer had fallen to a point where even individuals could buy one.

Professional writers began using microcomputers instead of typewriters. Businesses began using them instead of keeping records on punched cards. And students began using them as tutors. The ability of microcomputers to be programmed for "video games" helped draw attention to them. At the same time, their more workaday uses in the family were becoming recognized.

WHAT IS A COMPUTER?

Any device that helps people to find the answer to a problem can be called a computer. However, through the rest of the book, the term *computer* will refer to electronic devices that store, retrieve, and process information.

When a computer stores information (called *data*), it holds data in a *memory*. Once someone has put data into the computer, the data will stay there until something is done to the memory.

A person who retrieves data takes the data out of the computer in some way. Only stored data can be retrieved.

Computers also process data; they solve problems with the data. The data can be numbers or words. Using a computer to process data is like using a calculator combined with a typewriter.

Computers are made useful by instructions that are called *programs*. Most of the things that a computer can do can also be done by hand. But the computer does them more quickly, more

The world's first 32-bit, single-chip central processing unit, to be used in a desktop computer.

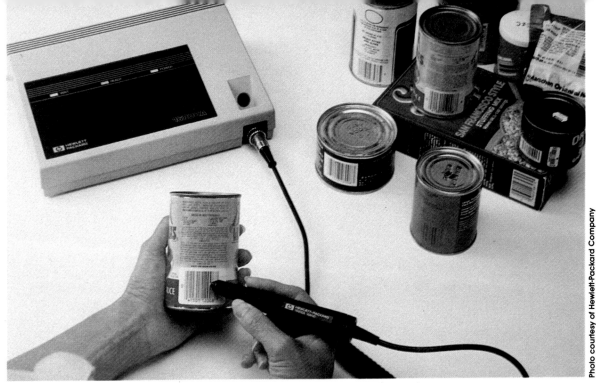

Some computers are used for only one purpose, like keeping track of prices at grocery stores.

consistently, and often more safely.

To be truly useful, a computer needs to be connected to other devices that allow data to be given to it (*inputted*) to be stored, or to be retrieved from it. The usual means of inputting data is with some type of keyboard. The data stored in a computer can be printed out in readable form on paper or recorded on a magnetic disk or tape.

Some computers are designed for only one kind of work. An electronic cash register is one example.

Most computers can be used for many kinds of work. They come in many shapes and sizes. But all computers are alike in one way: they use electronic switches to record data. A piece of data takes the form of a string of 1's and 0's. Because computers work with only those two digits, computers are called digital machines or tools.

The more switches that a computer has, the more useful it

can be. A computer having 1,000 electronic switches can record that many 1's and 0's. Most computers have several thousand switches; some have a million or more.

Each 1 or 0 stored in a computer is called a *bit* (*bi*nary digi*t*). Most computers handle the bits in groups of 8 or 16. A group of 4 bits is called a *nybble*. A group of 8 bits is called a *byte*.

A coding system that uses only 1's and 0's is called a binary system. When a computer is given data to record, it converts the information to a binary "string" of 1's and 0's and stores the string by turning switches on and off. An "off" switch equals a 0, and an "on" switch equals 1.

Because a computer can store information, its network of electronic switches is called its memory. A computer's ability to "remember" huge amounts of data is its most important feature.

For a computer to be useful, it needs to be able to recognize the letters of the alphabet, numerals, and several simple commands. The most common way is

through a set of codes called the American Standard Code for Information Interchange (ASCII). There are 128 of them. The most common way of entering the codes into a computer is with a typewriter-like keyboard. An ASCII keyboard is one that can send all 128 of the ASCII codes to the computer. Each ASCII code represents a letter of the alphabet, a number, a punctuation mark, or another symbol or command used in writing and calculating.

When a key is pressed, a signal is sent to the computer. The computer changes each ASCII character to a string of seven bits. There are 128 ASCII characters because there are 128 possible combinations of 1's and 0's, from 0000000 to 1111111. Each combination stands for a decimal number from 0 to 127.

When the letter *b* is pressed on a computer's keyboard, the computer converts the decimal number that stands for *b* (98) into a binary string—1100010. The computer also tacks on an extra 0 or 1 at the left end of the string as a marker to show where the string ends. The computer uses 8 bits (or 1 byte) to stand for an ASCII character.

The computer stores the string of 8 bits representing b in a specific place (the "address") in its electronic memory. An 8-bit computer is one that handles one byte at a time for processing. A 16-bit computer can handle two bytes at a time, and therefore can process data at a faster speed.

A computer has two kinds of memory. The manufacturer of the computer will build in a permanent memory. Whenever the computer is turned on, it follows the instructions contained in the permanent memory. The

Computer CPUs manage many different inputs and outputs.

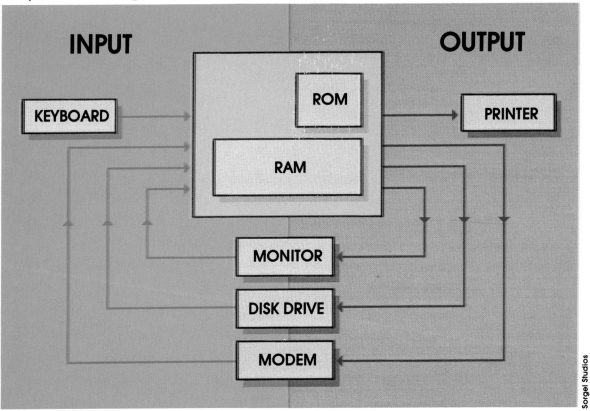

instructions cannot be changed. They are in the *read-only memory* (ROM).

The computer will also have a larger memory used to record information. It is called *random-access memory* (RAM). Anything stored in RAM will be lost (or forgotten) when the computer is turned off or when the supply of electricity to the computer is stopped for any reason. To preserve information stored in RAM, the user transfers it to a form that does not depend on constant electrical current. The information can be stored on a magnetic tape or disk, or on a punched tape. Or it can be printed in readable form on paper.

By itself, a computer can do nothing. It is only a network of miniature electronic circuits and switches. To get a computer to perform any work, it must be given a special set of instructions. The permanent instructions that the manufacturer places in the computer's ROM circuits prepare the computer to receive other instructions.

A set of instructions or commands that makes a computer useful is called a *program*. What a person can do with a program depends upon its design. Programs can be used to keep records, write essays, balance accounts, play video games, calculate weather patterns, and so forth. Most programs are designed to do one kind of task. A few can do two or three different kinds of work, using the same set of instructions.

A program tells the computer's *central processing unit* (CPU) what to do with the data that it receives. When a program is entered into the computer's RAM, the CPU can then follow the program's instructions. Each program gives the computer special abilities that it does not have by itself. For example, an accounting program turns a computer into an accounting machine. A word processing program turns the computer into a writing machine.

There is little standardization among computers. That is, the same program usually doesn't work in two different brands of computers. Every make of computer is somewhat different in its circuitry and manner of operation. Computers differ because they use different miniature circuits, called chips, in their CPUs. For example, the CPU of one 8-bit computer might be based on the Intel 8080 chip; another, on the MOS Technology 6502 chip; yet another, on the Zilog Z-80 chip.

Another thing that makes one computer different from other computers is a special program called its *disk-operating system* (DOS). Two different makes of computer might both be based on the Zilog Z-80 chip but have different DOSs. Their operating systems might be very similar, but the small differences might mean that a program will work well on one of them but not at all on the other. Those who write programs for computers (they are called programmers) have to know exactly how both the CPU and the DOS of each computer handle data.

When you use a computer, you are not aware of the operating system and do not see its digital workings. Instead, you use a program designed to get a computer to process information. Your program is then "translated" by another program (the operating system) and by the set of instructions in the computer's permanent memory (ROM).

The DOS provides ways in which data can be transmitted to the computer's CPU—from a magnetic disk, for example, or from a keyboard. The operating system also provides ways in which data stored in RAM can be displayed or recorded—on a video screen, for example, or on a magnetic disk. The operating system is often called the input/output (I/O) system. It is like a housekeeper or traffic policeman inside the computer.

How much a computer can do is limited by three things: the size of its memory, the abilities of each program written for it, and the design of its operating system. For example, an 8-bit computer can hold no more than 65,536 bytes in its RAM. A program designed for it might be limited in the number of records that it can handle at one time. And the computer's operating system might limit the size of the programs that can be used on it.

The physical size of a computer is not a safe way to judge what it can do. A small computer designed to be used by one person can do as many things, and do them as well, as the much larger, room-filling computers of the 1950s and 1960s.

Portable computers are as powerful today as room-sized ones were thirty years ago. They have become essential to people in business.

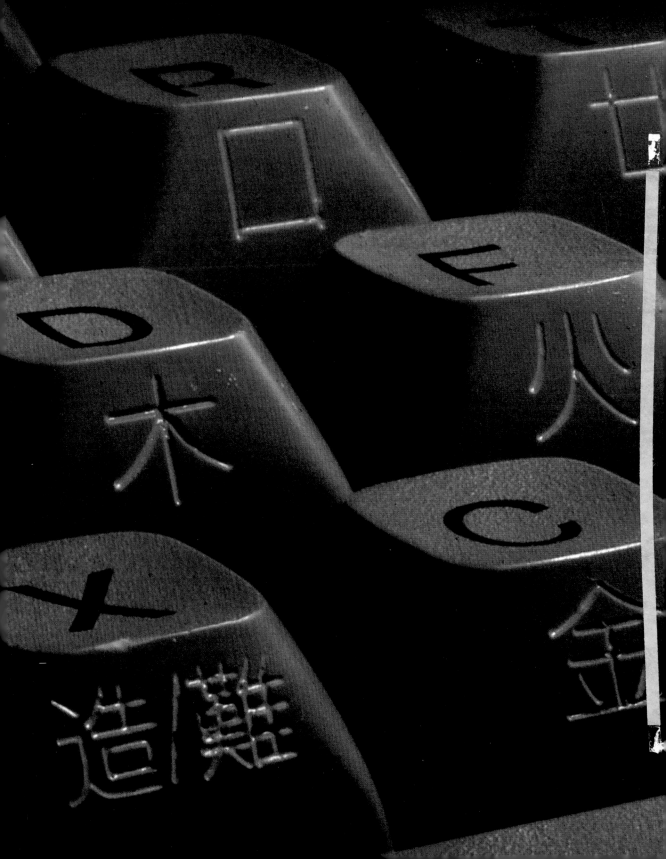

THE PARTS OF A PERSONAL COMPUTER

Strictly speaking, a computer consists only of the circuit board containing the central processing unit (CPU). The circuit board is often called the *motherboard*. Memory circuits controlled by the CPU might be mounted on the motherboard or on separate circuit boards connected to it.

The CPU needs to be given "directions" so that it can take in, process, and retrieve data on request. Attached to the computer are various ways of giving information to it and receiving information from it. The attachments are called *peripherals*—they "surround" the computer and make it useful. A computer and its peripherals make up a "computer system." A typical computer system includes, besides the computer, a *disk drive*, a *keyboard*, and a *monitor*.

Disk Drive

A disk drive records data on a magnetic disk or reads information from it. If a computer has two disk drives, one is called

The keyboards of computers have been designed for many languages around the world. Computer companies can customize the equipment for use in any country.

"A" and the other "B."

The disk drive is the most common method of recording information held in a computer's random-access memory (RAM). When the computer is turned off, any data stored in its RAM is lost. The disk drive records a copy of what is in the computer's memory and makes it available for later use.

One type of disk is the floppy disk or diskette. A floppy disk is a thin circle of plastic, 8 or 5¼ inches in diameter. It is coated with iron oxide and packaged inside a flexible sleeve that protects it from fingerprints and dust. The iron-oxide coating acts as a magnetic memory. One 8-inch floppy disk can record one million bytes or more.

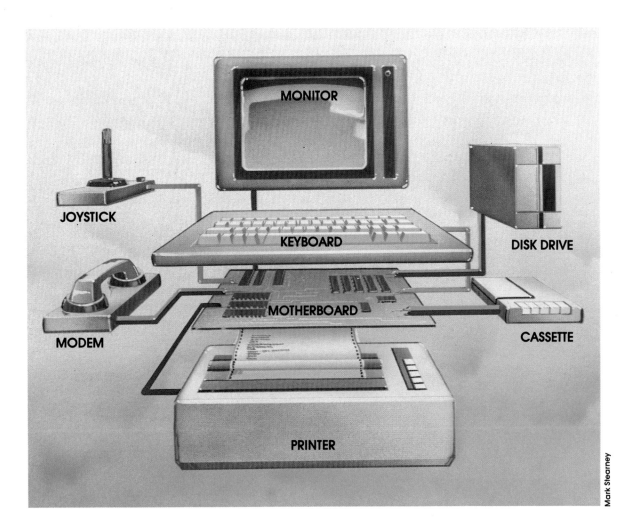

A "hard disk" is an aluminum disk encased in a dustproof drive. At least five million bytes can be recorded on a hard disk.

Some computers store data on cassette tapes or reels of magnetic tape rather than on disks. A disk drive can record and find information quicker than a tape recorder can.

A special type of memory that is sometimes used is a *bubble memory*. A bubble memory is an electronic chip that records digital data. (There are no bubbles involved, despite its name.) A bubble memory has many advantages: It is very durable, needs very little electrical power, keeps all the information recorded in it indefinitely, and is small in size. Bubble memories are especially useful in portable computers.

Keyboard

The part of a computer that gets the most use is the keyboard. A microcomputer receives most of the information that it is to process from its keyboard. The keys look like those on an electric typewriter. But there are usually special keys like ESCAPE and CONTROL , and special characters like ⌃, ⟨ , ⟩, and ⟍. Some keyboards have function keys, such as DELETE , or keys whose meaning the user can define.

Monitor

Most computers also come with a monitor—a video screen that can display sharp images of letters and numbers. When using a computer keyboard, the typed words appear on the monitor screen. The words can be changed easily, corrected, moved around, or erased. On the screen is a *cursor,* which is an underline or a block showing where the next typed character will appear. The keyboard may have special keys for moving the cursor's position on the screen.

The computer makes the keyboard and monitor act like an electronic typewriter. When the keyboard and monitor are separate from the computer, they are called

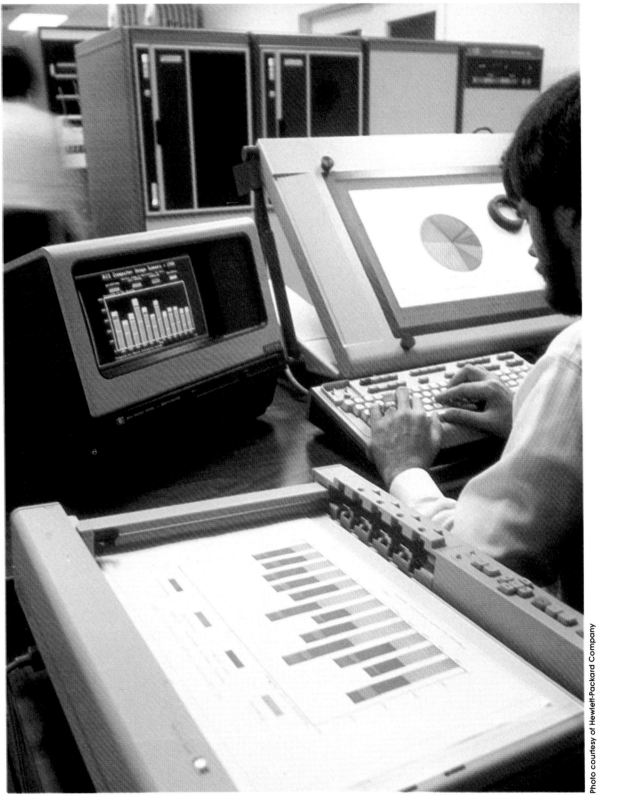

a video display terminal (VDT), or simply a terminal.

Other Peripherals

To get the monitor's electronic image printed on paper, the characters usually have to be stored on a disk first. They can then be transmitted by the computer from the disk to a *printer*. Printers designed to be used with computers operate at speeds ranging from 10 to 400 characters (letters, numbers, spaces, signs) per second.

A common use of computers is to transmit information via telephone lines to other computers. The device that allows them to do that is called a *modem*. A modem changes the computer's digital data (a stream of 1's and 0's) into two tones that will travel well over telephone lines. At the other end of the line, another modem changes the tones back into digital signals for the receiving computer. (The word *modem* is short for *mo*dulator-*de*modulator.)

Other kinds of peripherals have

A digitizer makes it possible to design models of things, like human-powered sailplanes.

been developed for special purposes. An *electronic tablet* is a flat surface that can be drawn upon with a special pen. Whatever is drawn on the tablet appears on the monitor screen.

Another example of a special-purpose peripheral is the *mouse*, a rectangular box about the size of a deck of cards. The mouse is used to move the cursor quickly to any position on the monitor screen. A mouse may have one or more keys that can be used to send messages to the computer, such as, "Get the accounting program."

Scientists use many different kinds of peripheral devices with

Words, numbers, and charts and graphs can be combined quickly and easily by using a computer. They can be made even more effective by using color. Printing the colored charts and graphs explains ideas very well.

computers. Special sensor devices are connected to computers and used for such things as detecting earthquakes, watching active volcanoes, measuring nuclear radiation, and studying a person's heartbeat.

Microcomputers and their peripherals are packaged in various ways. Some have the keyboard, monitor, and disk drives in a single unit. Others have the computer circuits and disk drives in one casing, connected to the keyboard and monitor by cables attached to sockets called "ports." Other ports are provided for the attachment of a printer and other peripherals. The ports are often called input/output (I/O) ports. They are connected to the computer's CPU and are controlled by the disk-operating system (DOS). The operating system tells the CPU how to handle data coming from and going to the peripherals.

The computer and its attachments are called "hardware." The programs—on

Hospitals use special equipment to measure an unborn baby's heart rate and oxygen supply. The equipment is run by a computer.

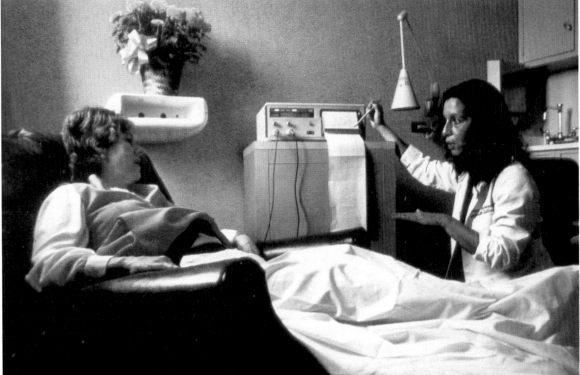

disks, cartridges, or other storage systems—that get the hardware to do useful work are called "software." The difference between hardware and software is sometimes not clear-cut. As we have seen, the CPU (hardware) comes with built-in programming (software) in its read-only memory (ROM).

New kinds of peripherals are constantly being invented as people find new uses for computers.

Computer hardware is put together and tested by people in assembly lines.

Millions of dollars are spent each year in the research of new ideas in science. Computers have helped in laser research and in other areas.

CONTROLLING THE COMPUTER

When working with a computer, you actually go through a program designed to make use of the computer's electronic circuits. The program has commands that will make the computer do some kind of task. A store owner might use an accounting program to keep track of earnings and expenses. A writer would use an editing or word-processing program to write letters or books or any other kind of material.

Programs that instruct a computer's central processing unit (CPU) may come recorded on a floppy disk. The program is "read into" the computer's memory by way of a disk drive. It is handled by another kind of program—the computer's disk-operating system (DOS).

Just as a train can ride only on tracks as wide apart as its wheels, a program will work only on a certain operating system. Most computers have only one DOS, and they will accept only those programs which are written for that DOS. Programs are usually

Artists use computers to create visuals for slides, films, and other media.

The original manuscript for this chapter was composed on a computer. Then it was edited.

sold in different versions for the different operating systems.

Some common types of operating systems are called CP/M, MS-DOS, UCSDp, and UNIX. A look at CP/M will describe in general how the others work within a computer.

CP/M, which stands for *Control Program for Microprocessors*, is widely used in microcomputers. The basic CP/M instructions are stored on a ROM chip, which is connected to the circuits of the computer's motherboard. The instructions tell the computer what to do when it is turned on, how to display characters on the monitor, how to send data to a printer or other peripheral, how to operate the disk drives, and how to send data to the memory circuits. They also tell the CPU what to do when a user enters a program. The program may be for accounting,

Type for this chapter was set from the edited manuscript using a computer-assisted typesetting machine.

check-writing, data-filing, games, or just about anything.

The programs that a user sends to the computer's memory are called *applications programs.* Most applications programs are written in one of the special programming languages.

Programming languages are ways of "speaking" to a computer. A computer can only accept instructions written in particular words and in a certain order. Otherwise the CPU will not "understand" the program. Programming languages can look very strange.

Some programming languages use commands that are English words, like **PRINT** and **STORE** and **DO**. These are called high-level languages. Some of the more commonly used high-level languages are **BASIC**, **FORTRAN**, and **COBOL**.

BASIC (*B*eginner's *A*ll-Purpose *S*ymbolic *I*nstruction *C*ode) was developed at Dartmouth College. It is a simplified version of a more complex language called FORTRAN (*for*mula *trans*lator). FORTRAN is usually used for writing programs for mathematicians and scientists. COBOL (*com*mon *b*usiness-*o*riented *l*anguage) is often used for writing business programs.

Once an applications program has been written in high-level language, a computer still cannot make any sense out of it. The program needs to be translated into the binary code (machine language). A *compiler* changes the program language into machine language.

A programmer could also write a program in a "low-level" assembly language. The low-level language is translated into machine language by an assembler program. For example, a computer's operating-system code for "jump to another memory location" might be 1100011. The programmer can write JMP instead, and the assembler program converts JMP to 1100011.

In many cases, the person using a computer is actually using an applications program. The applications program is changed by another program (the disk-operating system) and then translated into machine language (1's and 0's). The compiler that changes the program is built into the computer's read-only memory (ROM).

Here's how the process might

Circuits of a computer hold its memory and all of the information that it needs to run.

work with a specific program. Suppose the computer has two disk drives—A and B—and a keyboard with monitor connected to it. When you turn on the computer, the operating system sends a message to the monitor screen: "Place a program disk in drive A and press RETURN." Then insert a floppy disk into drive A.

The disk contains a program designed to keep track of names and addresses. The program prepares the CPU to process, store, and retrieve names and addresses in a specific way. The operating system "reads" the program from the disk in drive A and passes it on to the CPU through the compiler. The CPU stores the program in its memory circuits and also remembers what is stored where. The program is then ready for use.

The floppy disk that contains your personal address file goes into drive B. You can ask for a blank-address form on the monitor screen by typing a

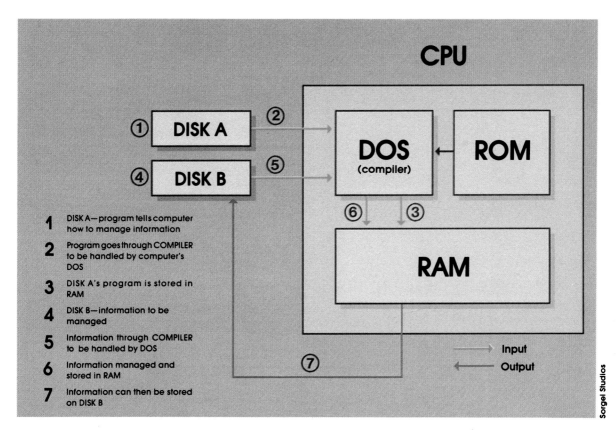

1 DISK A—program tells computer how to manage information

2 Program goes through COMPILER to be handled by computer's DOS

3 DISK A's program is stored in RAM

4 DISK B—information to be managed

5 Information through COMPILER to be handled by DOS

6 Information managed and stored in RAM

7 Information can then be stored on DISK B

command on the keyboard. The computer will then clear the monitor screen. It will show the form that you designed when you first started the file. It might look like this:

Name:
Address:
City:
State:
Zip:

You now can type in the data— names and addresses of some new friends. The program will allow you to type them one at a time. Command keys tell the program system to store the names and addresses temporarily and to give you another blank form after each one is entered.

When you have finished typing the last name and address into a form, you type in another command. It causes the computer to take the new names and addresses from its memory circuits and to record them at the end of the address file on the floppy disk in drive B.

Usually, a computer does not have to work very hard when it is processing words like name-and-address files. Other types of programs are very lengthy and complicated. They get the computer to perform very difficult processing tasks. Computers perform most tasks so quickly that they seem to be done instantly. However, some kinds of processing may take anywhere from a few seconds to several minutes.

Some programs are like two or three different programs in one. For example, there are programs that can be used for financial analysis, record keeping, and graphics. Such programs are referred to as integrated software.

Some programs allow computers to be used in unusual ways. For example, there are computers that have special monitors with screens that are sensitive to touch. Just the touch of a finger on one part of the screen activates the CPU. For example, you may choose what part of a program you want to use by touching the screen over a description of that part or a picture of what that part does.

With some computers, images can be drawn on the monitor screen with a "light pen." Other computers can respond to simple voice-commands, such as "store file on disk B" or "next screen." These computers have very large memories so that they can use the lengthy programs that make such special abilities possible.

Writing an applications program is both a science and an art. It is a science because getting a computer to process data requires knowledge of another language and very logical thinking. Every possibility must be thought through. Writing computer programs is difficult, detailed work.

Writing programs is also an art. The programmer needs to be able to make a program complex and powerful and easy to use at the same time.

Some monitors have screens that are sensitive to the touch. Data can be moved from one place to another with the touch of a finger.

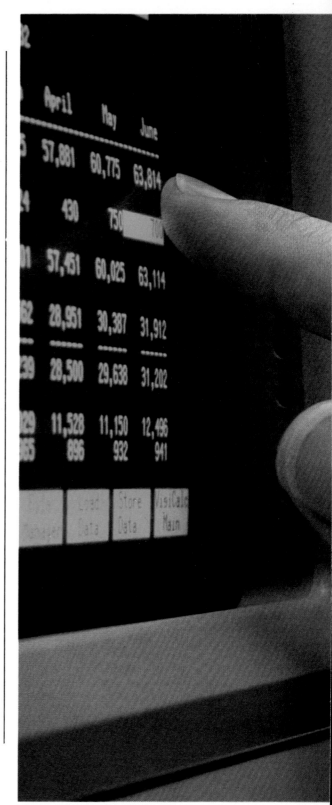

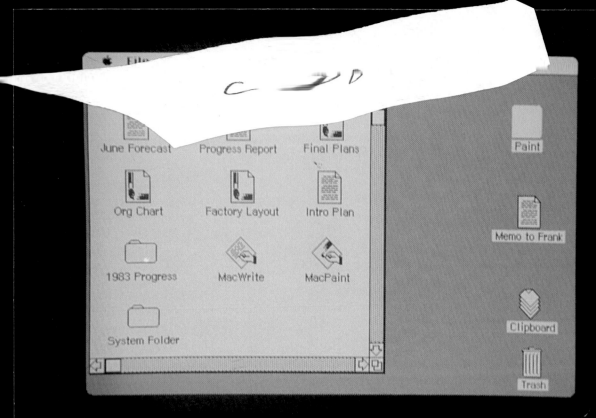

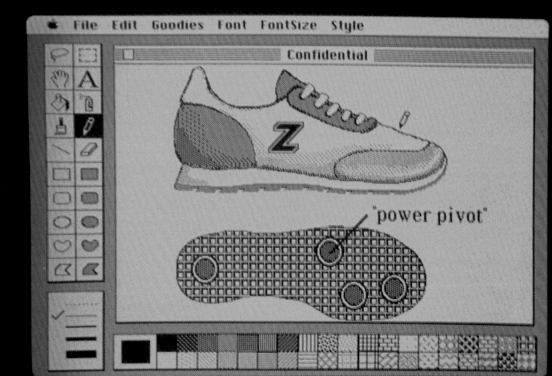

USES OF PERSONAL COMPUTERS

Personal computers are capable of many different kinds of operations.

What a computer can do depends on the program that is loaded into its memory. There are thousands of programs available for use on personal computers. Some programs will work on many computers. Other programs are designed for one particular computer.

Computer programs fall into several categories, based on the type of work that they make possible. A word-processing program turns a computer into an electronic typewriter. A graphics program makes it possible to draw graphs, charts, and other pictures on the monitor screen.

Learning to use a computer is mostly learning to use different programs. Each program provides fairly simple ways to do whatever it is designed to do. In most cases, there will be a set of commands that can be typed on the keyboard. A word-processing program has ways to do such things as delete words, insert words, move words, and underline words. A budgeting program has ways to set up a statement of future expenses and may also print checks, keep tax records, and store a list of family possessions.

Word processing is one of the more common types of program for personal computers. Any kind of writing that is lengthy and involves careful revision can be done more easily with a word-processing program than in any other way. The monitor screen is like a chalkboard, only better: changes are easily made, and even paragraphs can be moved from one place to another in the written text. When the changes are completed, the text can be printed on paper. The text can also be stored as a magnetic recording on a floppy disk. Later, it can be checked, revised, and printed again without having to be retyped.

Personal computers are also used for keeping track of money. Businesses use them to keep records of amounts spent,

Fuel-indicating systems of a jet are tested using color graphics and a light pen. The graphics simulate the meters in the jet's cockpit.

Photo courtesy of Hewlett-Packard Company

People of all ages are able to use computers to help them to learn. Computers can ask questions, keep track of answers, and help people learn new things.

amounts earned, and amounts paid in wages and taxes. Accountants use them to calculate the value of investments. Banks use them to have available the current amount held in savings and checking accounts.

Personal computers are used in schools and colleges for many purposes. There are many educational programs. Some give practice in arithmetic or grammar. Others help students master such subjects as typing, bookkeeping, and computer programming. Still others help prepare students for tests.

Some personal computers can play game programs. Games act as tests of players' reaction times and abilities to solve puzzles. Games also test coordination and concentration. Some are simply card and board games transferred onto a video screen. Some can be played with only a keyboard; others require the use of special peripherals called joysticks.

One of the more useful things that a computer can do is to reduce paperwork. The contents of all of the records in a file drawer can be stored on one floppy disk. A hard disk can store the contents of several file cabinets. Such records are easier to find with a data-management program than they would be if they existed only on paper in a file folder.

Another common use of the computer is to communicate with other computers. There are several computer *data bank* services available. A data bank is a storehouse of information. A computer data bank is like a library that gives information to computers. The user connects a computer to one of the services through telephone lines. The computer connects to the telephone lines through a modem.

There are data banks (or bases) for just about any kind of information that a person could want. They include stocks, weather, agricultural news, futures markets, games, world

news, and sports. You can even shop with a computer.

One data bank contains all of the articles of an encyclopedia. You could obtain a copy of its article on "Japan" or "Molecule" by asking for it by name. The data bank transmits the text of the article to your computer's memory, and the computer records it on a floppy disk. It can also be read on the monitor. The exchanging of files between computers is possible with a communications program.

```
AT KEY CORN AND SOYBEAN BELT LOCATIONS,
IN CENTS PER BUSHEL, BASIS CHICAGO
FUTURES, EXCEPT FOR HARD RED WINTER
WHEAT, WHICH IS BASIS KANSAS CITY
FUTURES. CHANGES ARE IN COMPARISON WITH
THE PREVIOUS MORNING'S BASIS LEVELS,
AND DO NOT REFLECT PROTECTION.

LOCATION        CORN            SOYBEANS
TOLEDO          - 4 DEC DN 1   -15 JAN DN 1
CINCINNATI      X 0 DEC DN 2   -12 JAN DN 2
INDIANAPOLIS    - 5 DEC UP 1   -20 JAN UNCH
DECATUR, ILL.   X 4 DEC DN 1   X 8 NOV UNCH
CHICAGO         X 3 DEC DN 4   - 8 JAN UNCH
PEORIA/PEKIN    X 5 DEC DN 3   -11 JAN UNCH
DAVENPORT       X 0 DEC DN 3   -13 JAN DN 3
DES MOINES      - 6 DEC DN 5   - 9 NOV UP 2
CEDAR RAPIDS    - 3 DEC DN 1   - 3 NOV UP 2
SIOUX CITY      - 9 DEC UNCH   -28 NOV UP 2
ST. LOUIS       X 4 DEC DN 3   X 2 NOV UP 2

<RET> for more or X <RET> to exit _
                        DCONN   NEXT
```

Agricultural market information from the AgriData Network data bank is one example of what a computer can receive as a terminal.

Art work can be made using computers. Animated films, video game screens, and commercials have been illustrated completely using computers and special drawing pads.

Also becoming more common is the use of computers for "electronic mail." A letter or report typed on a computer can be sent just about anywhere in the country by telephone. Then the letter can be printed and delivered by a mail service at the second location. Or it can be received directly by the person to whom it is addressed if that person has a computer and modem. Electronic mail is less expensive and faster than other ways of sending important information.

The uses of computers are limited, after all. They're limited by memory size and programmers' imaginations. But those limits are being expanded constantly, as are the uses that people make of computers.

45

PRONUNCIATION GUIDE

These symbols have the same sounds as the darker letters in the sample words.

ə	balloon, ago
a	map, have
ä	father, car
b	ball, rib
d	did, add
e	bell, get
ē	keen, leap
f	fan, soft
g	good, big
h	hurt, ahead
i	rip, ill
ī	side, sky
j	join, germ
k	king, ask
l	let, cool
m	man, same
n	no, turn
ō	cone, know
ȯ	all, saw
p	part, scrap
r	root, tire
s	so, press
sh	shoot, machine
t	to, stand
ü	pool, lose
u̇	put, book
v	view, give
w	wood, glowing
y	yes, year
′	accent

GLOSSARY

These words are defined the way they are used in the book.

ASCII abbreviation for American Standard Code for Information Interchange; a common set of codes used on digital computers

binary number (bī′ nə rē nəm′ bər) a number expressed as a series of 1's and 0's

bit (bit′) a *bi*nary digi*t*, equal to 1 or 0; used in computers to encode information and commands

byte (bīt′) a group of bits, usually eight, used to encode a character

central processing unit (sen′ trəl präs′ es ing yü′ nət) (CPU) the main portion of a computer's electronic circuits

chip (chip′) an integrated circuit etched on a small piece of silicon, equal to about 10,000 transistors and other electronic components

cursor (kər′ sȯr) a small underline or rectangle on a video screen showing where the next typed character will appear

disk-operating system (disk′ ä′p′ ə rāt ing sis′ təm) (DOS) a program designed to tell a computer's central processing unit how to communicate with its peripherals; used on computers having one or more disk drives hardware (här′ dwar) the electronic circuits and attachments of a computer (See also *software*.)

integrated circuit (int′ ə grāt′ ed sər′ kət) a circuit that combines the abilities of several separate circuits in one, small electronic device (See also *chip*.)

machine language (mə shēn′ lang′ gwij) the internal language of a computer, represented as groups and strings of 1's and 0's

modem (mō′ dem) a *modulator-dem-odulator*; a device that changes the 1's and 0's of computer codes into two tones that travel along telephone lines

monitor (män′ ə tər) a video screen that can show letters, numbers, and other images clearly; the usual way of checking the data entered into, or stored in, a computer

motherboard (məth′ ər bōrd′) the main circuit board in a computer on which the central processing unit is mounted

nybble (nib′ əl) a group of four bits; half a byte (See also *bit*, *byte*.)

peripheral (pərif′ ə rəl) a device attached to a computer as a source of data or as a receiver of data

port (pōrt′) a plug-device that allows peripherals to be attached to a computer (See also *peripheral*.)

program (prō′ gram) a set of instructions that tell a computer to perform specific kinds of processing tasks

random-access memory (ran′ dəm ak′ ses mem′ ə rē) (RAM) memory circuits available to the user of a computer; they store data in byte-size groups, but lose the data if electrical power is turned off

read-only memory (rēd′ ōn′ lē mem′ ə rē) (ROM) memory circuits that are permanently programmed; data stored in ROM can be "read" but cannot be changed by the user of a computer

software (sòf′ twar) a computer program, distinct from hardware (See *program*, *hardware*.)

INDEX